Kindergarten Skills

MW01364510

Winter Fun Days

This book combines high-interest theme-based activities with practice in essential basic skills. The activities have been designed to provide practice and reinforcement for children in a variety of curriculum areas. You'll find practice in ABC's, math, vocabulary, writing, letter recognition, fine-motor skills, and more! Throughout the book you'll find appealing pages featuring winter animals and winter holidays. Students will enjoy exploring winter fun in all its facets.

Skills in this book include:

Counting to 10 • Recognizing money • Patterning • Vocabulary
Matching uppercase and lowercase letters • Inferences
Classification • ABC order

And more!

Written by **Catherine Hernandez, Marcia S. Gresko,** and **Vicky Shiotsu**

Cover illustration by **Sherry Neidigh**

Illustrated by **Susanne DeMarco, Ethel Gold, Joyce John, Sherry Neidigh,** and **Becky Radtke**

FS132912 Winter Fun Days

23740 Hawthorne Blvd.
Torrance, CA 90505

ISBN 0-7682-0390-2

Table of Contents
Skills & Concepts

My Favorite Winter Holiday
Writing 3

Animals in Winter
Counting 4

Winter Counting
Counting 5

Holiday Fun
Counting 6

Holiday Surprise
Numbers 1–10 7

Ready to Go
Ordering objects by size, Classifying 8

Letter Skate
Recognizing and writing alphabet letters 9

Mitten Match-up
Matching uppercase and lowercase letters 10

Comparing Things
Vocabulary 11

More Comparing
Vocabulary 12

Matching Words
Matching common words 13

Holiday Lights
Appreciating that people celebrate different holidays 14–17

A Special Day
Skill: Personal response 18

Find the Gift
ABC order 19

Count the Toys
Counting to 10 20

Evergreen Trees
Learning about evergreen trees 21

Holiday Patterns
Patterning 22

Looking at Coins
Recognizing a penny, a nickel, a dime 23

I Can Save Money
Identifying a penny, a nickel, a dime 24

I Can Buy Gifts
Exploring pennies and cents 25

Happy New Year
Counting to 10 26

Missing Numbers
Numbers 1–10 27

A New Friend
Alphabet recognition and order 28

Word Match
Matching phrases 29

Who Needs This?
Making inferences 30

Chinese New Year Fun
Matching numbers 31

Related Activities
Activity Suggestions 32

Name ______________________ Skill: Numbers 1–10

Holiday Surprise

Count from 1 to 10.
Connect the dots.

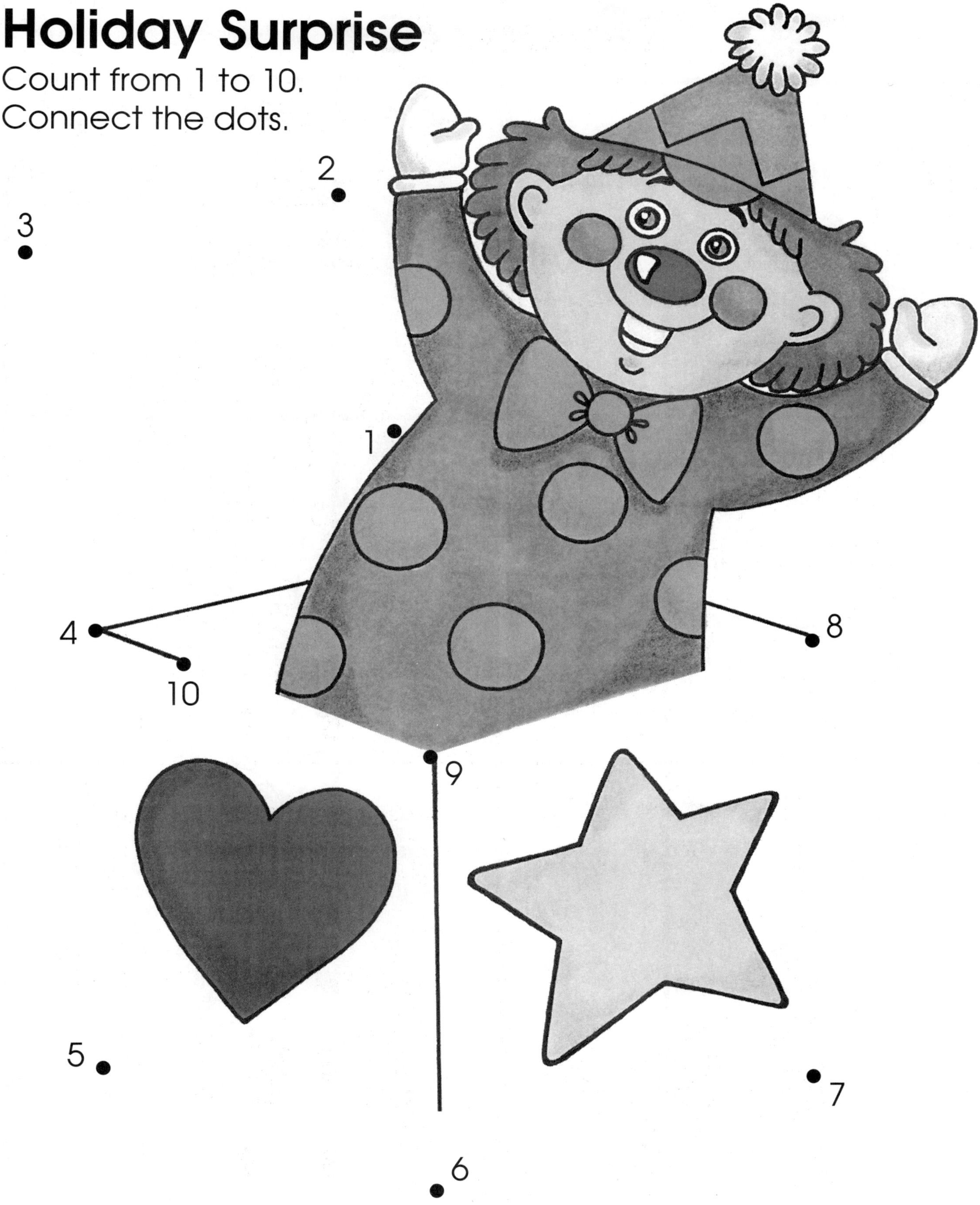

Name ____ Skill: Ordering objects by size, Classifying

Ready to Go

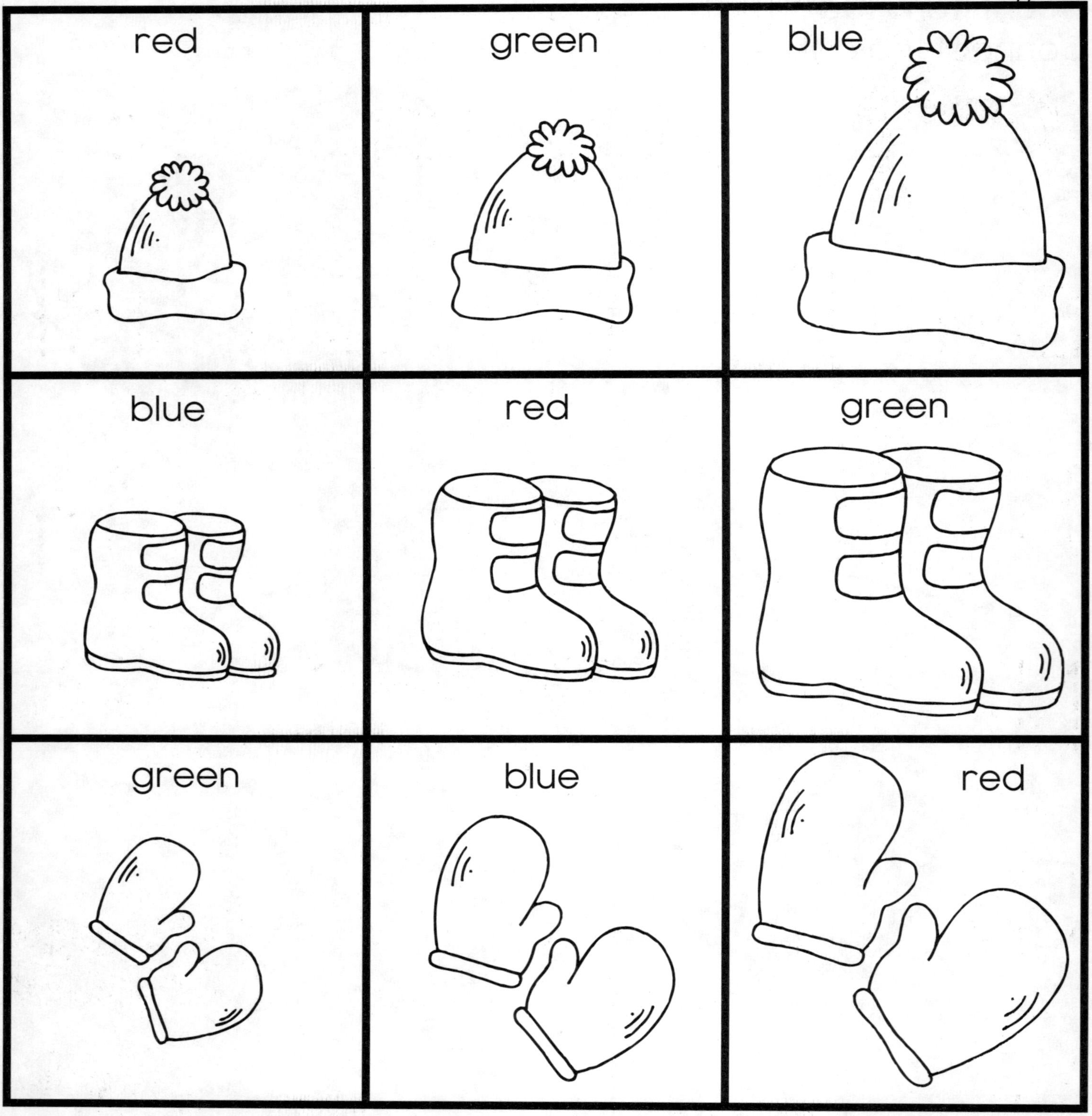

Activity Directions: Have students color the items, cut them out, and divide the cutouts into groups of items that are the same. Tell students to arrange the pictures in each set from smallest to biggest. Then have students arrange the pictures in each set from biggest to smallest. The cards can also be used for classifying (sorting) activities. Say, *Divide the cards into groups. You decide how to group them.* If necessary, help students divide the cards into groups based on one attribute, such as color. The cards can also be grouped according to size or kind of item. Let students explain how they grouped the cards.

Name ____________________

Skill: Recognizing and writing alphabet letters

Letter Skate

Trace the letters.

Aa Bb Cc

Dd Ee Ff Gg Hh

Ii Jj Kk Ll Mm

Nn Oo Pp Qq Rr

Ss Tt Uu Vv

Ww Xx Yy Zz

Name ______________________ Skill: Matching uppercase and lowercase letters

Mitten Match-up

Draw lines between the mittens to match up the letters.

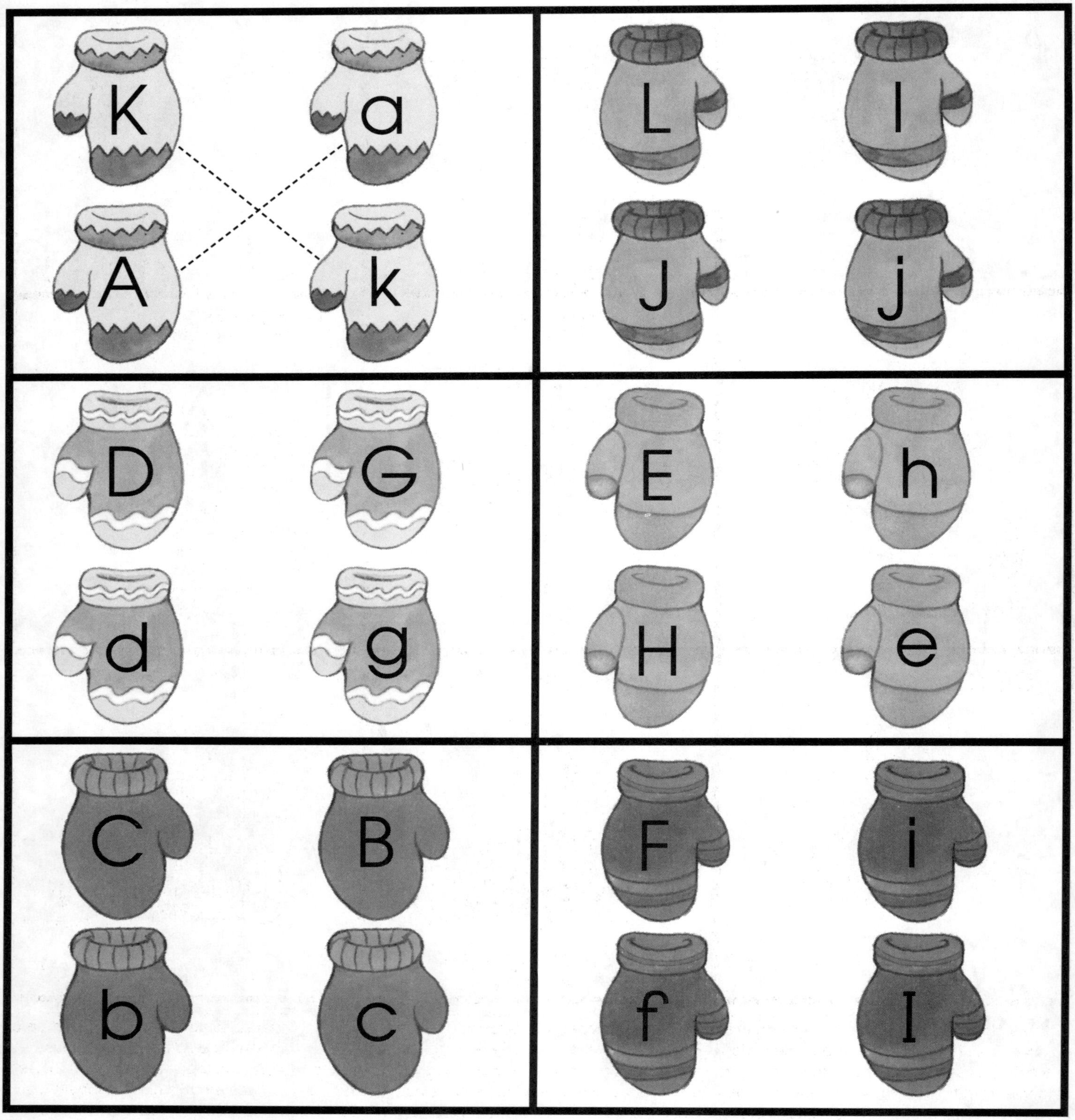

Name ____________________ Skill: Vocabulary

Comparing Things

Activity Directions: Use the pictures on this page with the pictures on page 12 to extend students' understanding of words that compare objects. First, have students group the matching pictures together (big, bigger, biggest; high, higher, highest; and so on). Then choose one set and have students find the card numbered 1. Read the word aloud. Have students find the next card in the set (numbered 2). Ask students how the picture is different from the one on the first card. Read the word aloud as students compare the two cards. Repeat the process for the third card. Finally, have students place all three cards in a row and read the words together. You may want to encourage students to make up sentences using the different words.

Name ____________________ Skill: Vocabulary

More Comparing

Activity Directions: Use the pictures on this page with the pictures on page 11 to extend students' understanding of words that compare objects. First, have students group the matching pictures together (heavy, heavier, heaviest; small, smaller, smallest; and so on). Then choose one set and have students find the card numbered 1. Read the word aloud. Have students find the next card in the set (numbered 2). Ask students how the picture is different from the one on the first card. Read the word aloud as students compare the two cards. Repeat the process for the third card. Finally, have students place all three cards in a row and read the words together. You may want to encourage students to make up sentences using the different words.

Name ____________________ Skill: Matching common words

Matching Words

In each row, circle the words that match the first one.

boy	box	boy	bog	boy
see	see	sea	see	set
run	rub	run	run	ran
cat	cat	car	cot	cat
on	no	on	in	on
girl	girl	gift	girl	gill
ball	hall	ball	ball	bell

Holiday Lights

Holiday Celebrations Around the World

This book belongs to ______________________________

Twinkle, twinkle, Hanukkah lights,
Lasting lights on happy nights. 1

Activity Directions: Cut this page in half, cut this section off, and staple together with pages 15–17 to make a holiday book.

Twinkle, twinkle, Las Posadas lights,
Searching lights on happy nights.

2

Twinkle, twinkle, Diwali lights,
Greeting lights on happy nights.

3

Activity Directions: Cut this page in half, cut this section off, and staple together with pages 14, 16, and 17 to make a holiday book.

Twinkle, twinkle, Kwanzaa lights,
Teaching lights on happy nights. 4

Twinkle, twinkle, St. Lucia lights,
Crowning lights on happy nights. 5

Activity Directions: Cut this page in half, cut this section off, and staple together with pages 14, 15, and 17 to make a holiday book.

Twinkle, twinkle, Christmas lights,
Sharing lights on happy nights.

6

Information About the Holidays

Light is an important part of holiday celebrations in many cultures.

Hanukkah—The Jewish Feast of Lights is celebrated for eight days and nights. Each night the menorah is lit. This commemorates a victory 2,000 years ago in which the Jews won freedom to worship their own God.

Las Posadas—Las Posadas is a Mexican Christmas holiday. On each of the nine nights before Christmas, a procession through the community reenacts Mary and Joseph's search for lodging.

Diwali—The Hindu Festival of Lights is a joyous Indian festival. Homes are decorated with hundreds of tiny lamps to welcome Lakshmi, the Hindu goddess of good fortune.

Kwanzaa—This African-American festival lasts seven days and celebrates families and traditional African values. Each night, a candle is lit in the kinara (candleholder), and a Kwanzaa principle is discussed.

St. Lucia's Day—St. Lucia's Day is a Swedish holiday honoring St. Lucia and reminding people that winter will come to an end. In the morning, the oldest daughter dons a white robe and a wreath of candles and serves coffee and buns to her family.

Christmas—Christmas is the Christian celebration of the birth of Jesus Christ. Candles and other lights are an important part of both religious and secular Christmas celebrations. Many people decorate homes and trees, and exchange gifts.

7

Activity Directions: Cut this page in half, cut this section off, and staple together with pages 14, 15, and 16 to make a holiday book.

Name ____________________ Skill: Personal response

A Special Day

Color the pictures that show things your family uses to celebrate a special holiday.

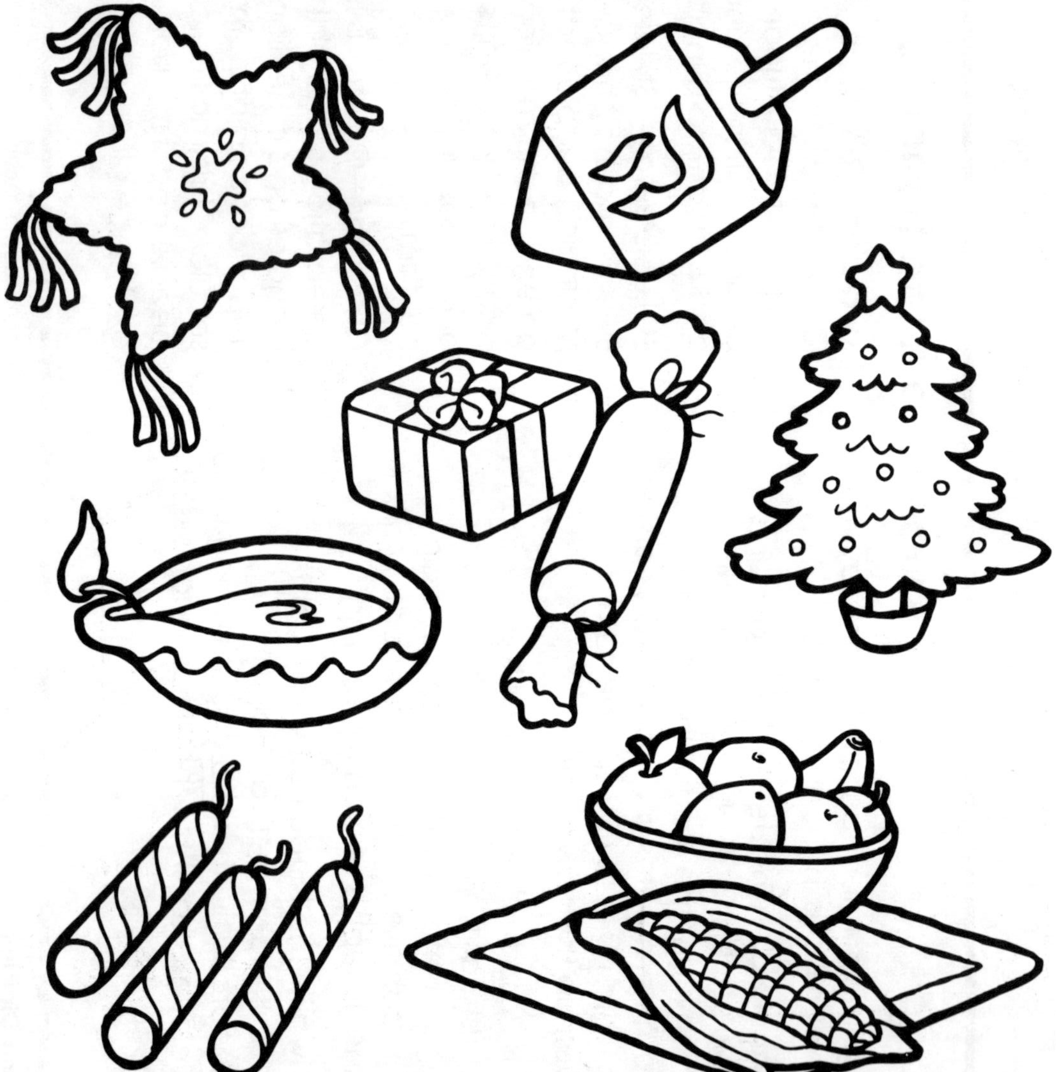

Color the child to look like you dressed for a special holiday.

Name ______________________________ Skill: ABC order

Find the Gift

Follow ABC order to help the kids find the gift.
Color the path.

Name ______________________________ Skill: Counting to 10

Count the Toys

Count. Write the number.

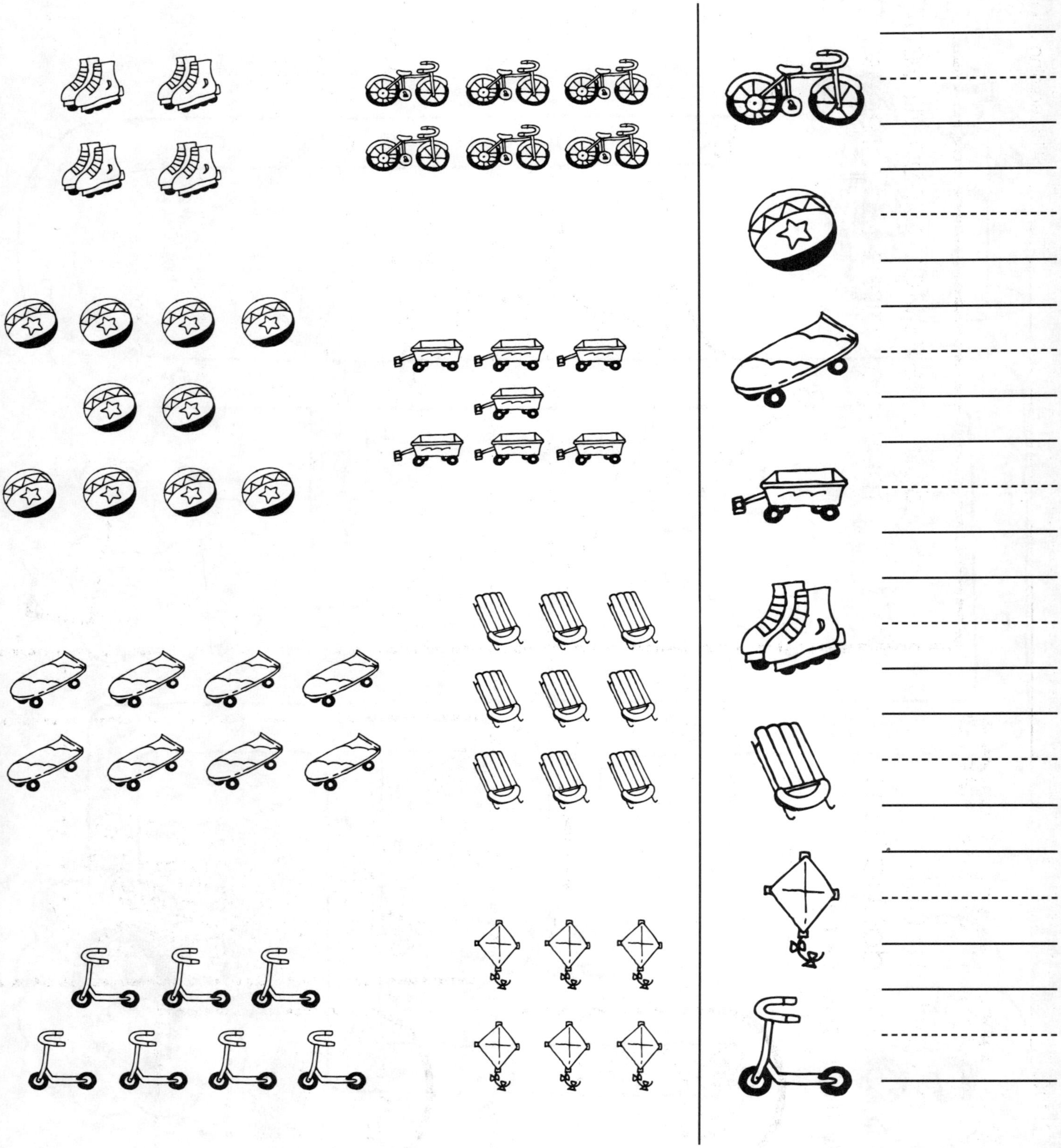

Name ______________________________ Skill: Learning about evergreen trees

Evergreen Trees

Color and cut out.
Fold on the dotted lines.
Match and paste.

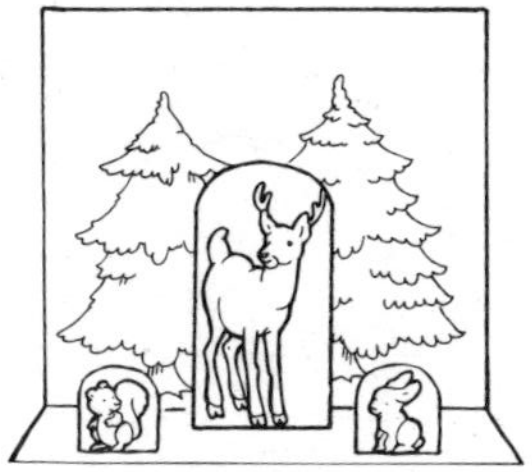

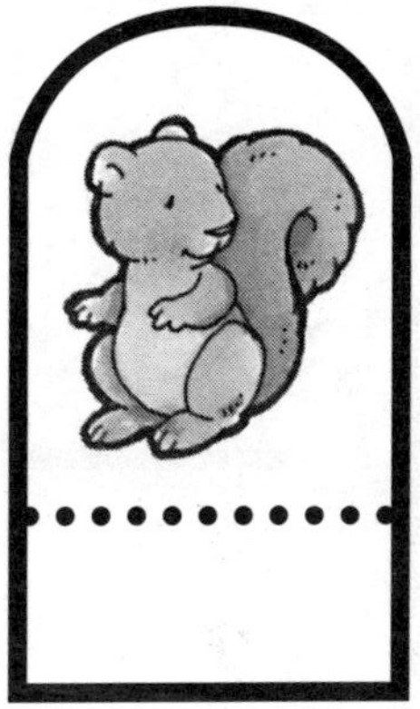

Some trees stay green all year.
They are called evergreens.

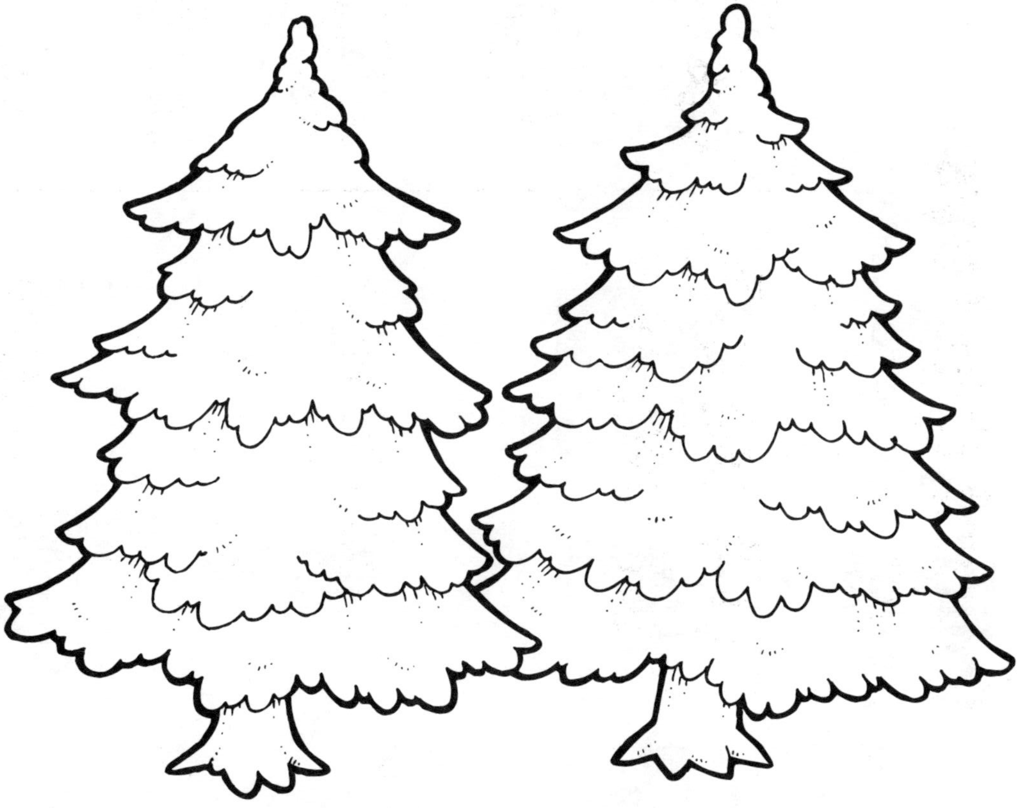

paste

paste

paste

Name ____ Skill: Patterning

Holiday Patterns

Cut and paste the correct picture to complete each pattern. Color the pictures.

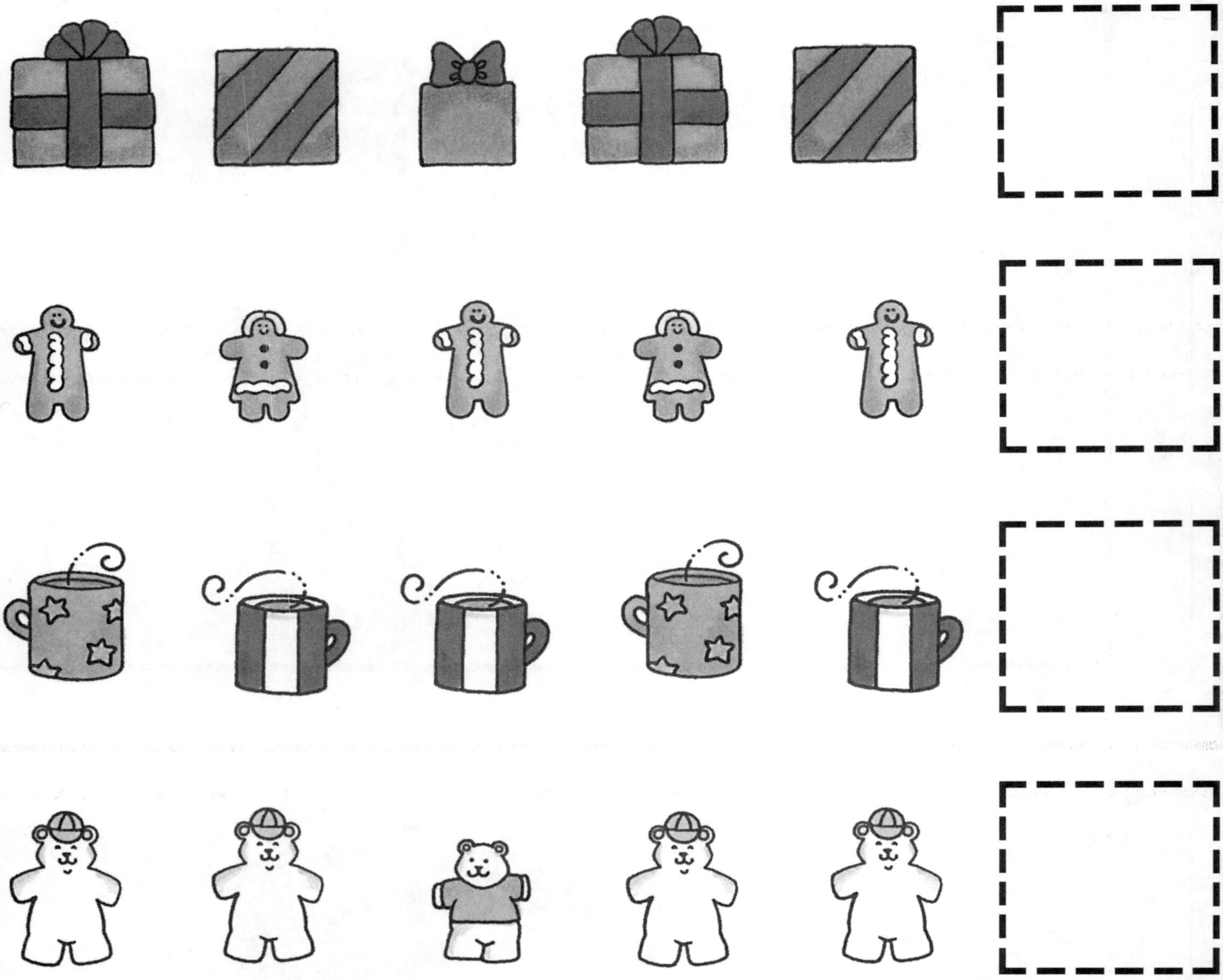

Name ____________________

Skill: Recognzing a penny, nickel, and dime

Looking at Coins

Cut, fold, and paste.

penny 1¢

head

penny 1¢

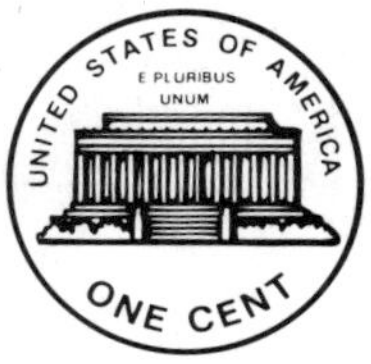

tail

nickel 5¢

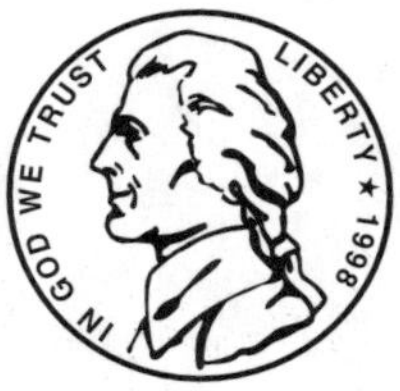

head

nickel 5¢

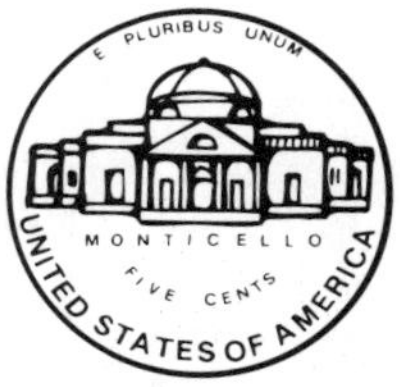

tail

dime 10¢

head

dime 10¢

tail

Activity Directions: After students have made the coin flashcards, discuss the two sides of these coins. (penny—Abraham Lincoln and the Lincoln Memorial; nickel—Thomas Jefferson and Monticello, the home Jefferson designed and built for himself; dime—Franklin D. Roosevelt and a torch with laurel and oak twigs.) Note: These coins are enlarged to better show their detail.

Name ______________________________________ Skill: Identifying a penny, a nickel, a dime

I Can Save Money

Color the piggy banks. Listen to your teacher for directions.

Activity Directions: Direct the students to put specific coins on a piggy bank, such as *Put a penny on the red piggy bank. Put two nickels on the blue piggy bank. Put a nickel and dime on the green piggy bank.* Then ask questions such as *How many pennies are on the red piggy bank? How many nickels are on the blue piggy bank?*

Name ______________________________________ Skill: Exploring money—pennies and cents

I Can Buy Gifts

Match the correct amount of pennies to each toy.

1 cent

2 cents

3 cents

4 cents

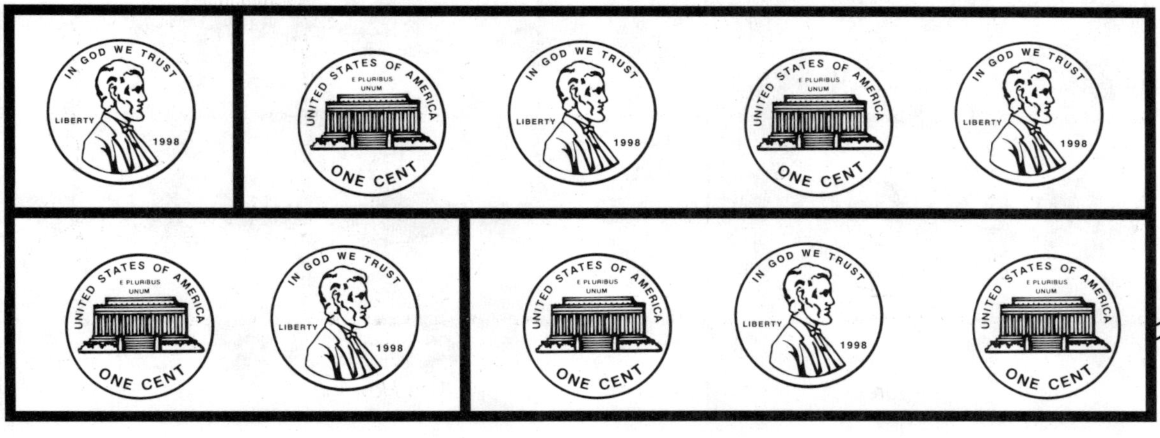

Name ______________________________ Skill: Counting to 10

Happy New Year

Count. Circle the number.

4 **5**

7 **8**

8 **9**

9 **10**

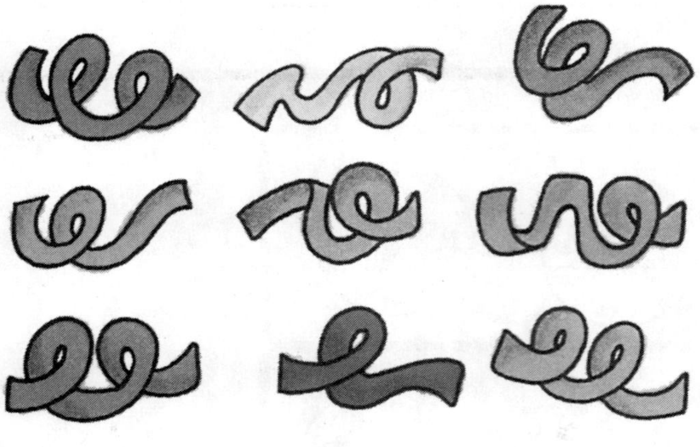

8 **9**

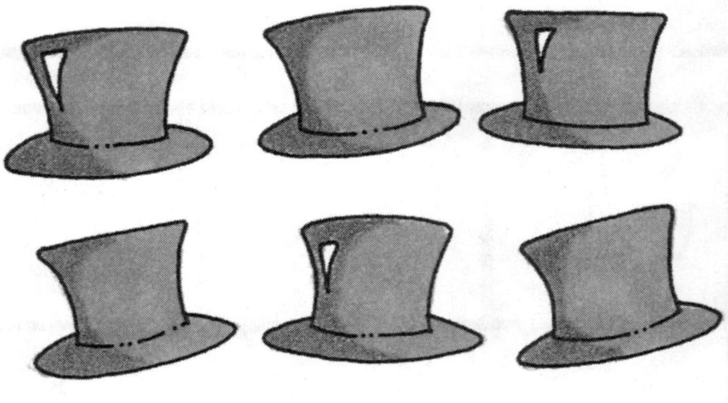

5 **6**

Name ____________________ Skill: Numbers 1 to 10

Missing Numbers

Color the numbers.

1 2 3 4 5

6 7 8 9 10

Write the numbers from 1 to 10.

1 ___ 3 4 ___

6 7 ___ 9 ___

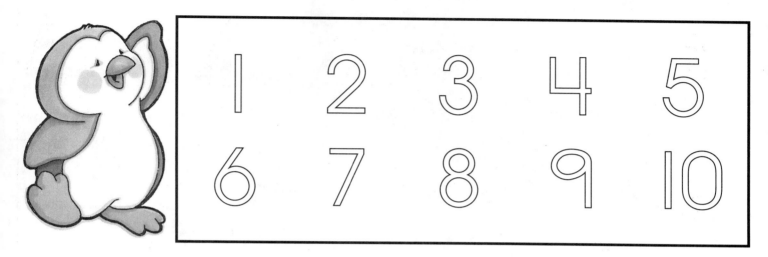

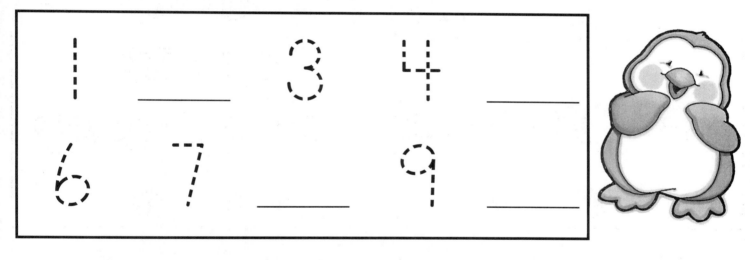

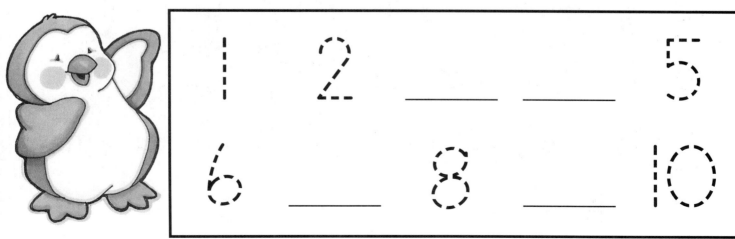

1 2 ___ ___ 5

6 ___ 8 ___ 10

Name ____________________ Skill: Alphabet recognition and order

A New Friend

Connect the dots from **a** to **z**.

Name ____________________ Skill: Matching phrases

Word Match

Circle the words that match the words at the top of each box.

red sled

red slide

red sled

fun ride

fun ride

fan ride

wet kid

well kid

wet kid

hot fire

hot fire

hot find

Name ____________________ Skill: Making inferences

Who Needs This?

Look at the first picture in each row.
Color the picture that shows who needs it.

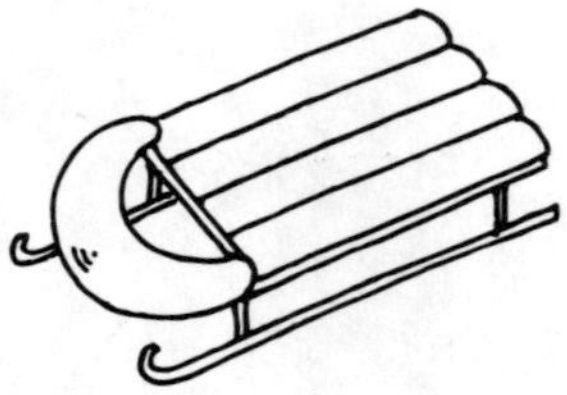

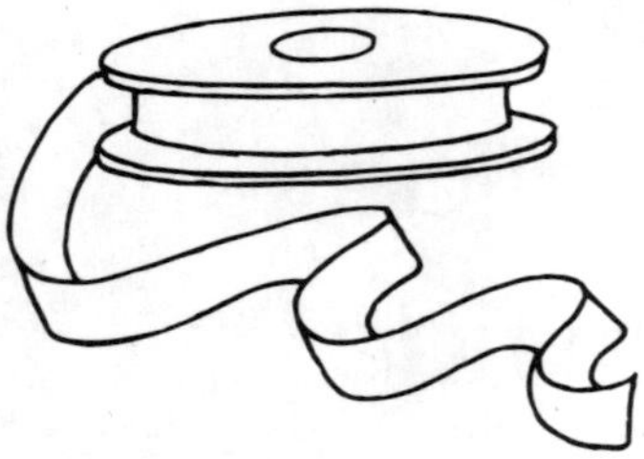

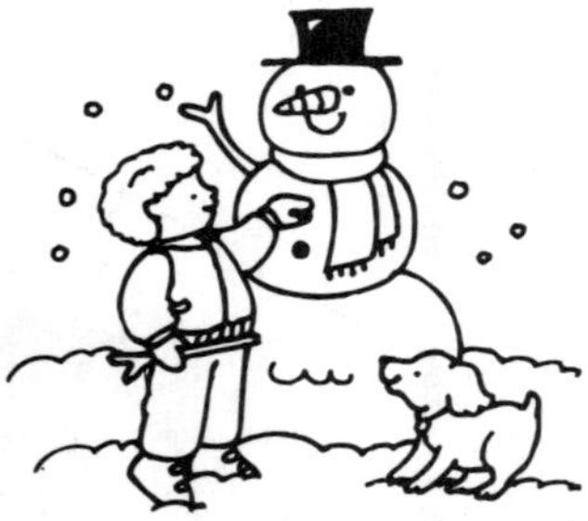
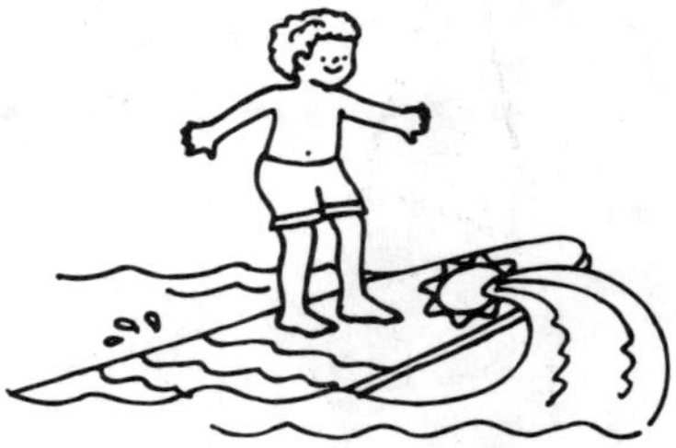

Name ______________________________ Skill: Matching numbers

Chinese New Year Fun

Color. Use the number key.

7 = green 8 = red 9 = blue 10 = yellow

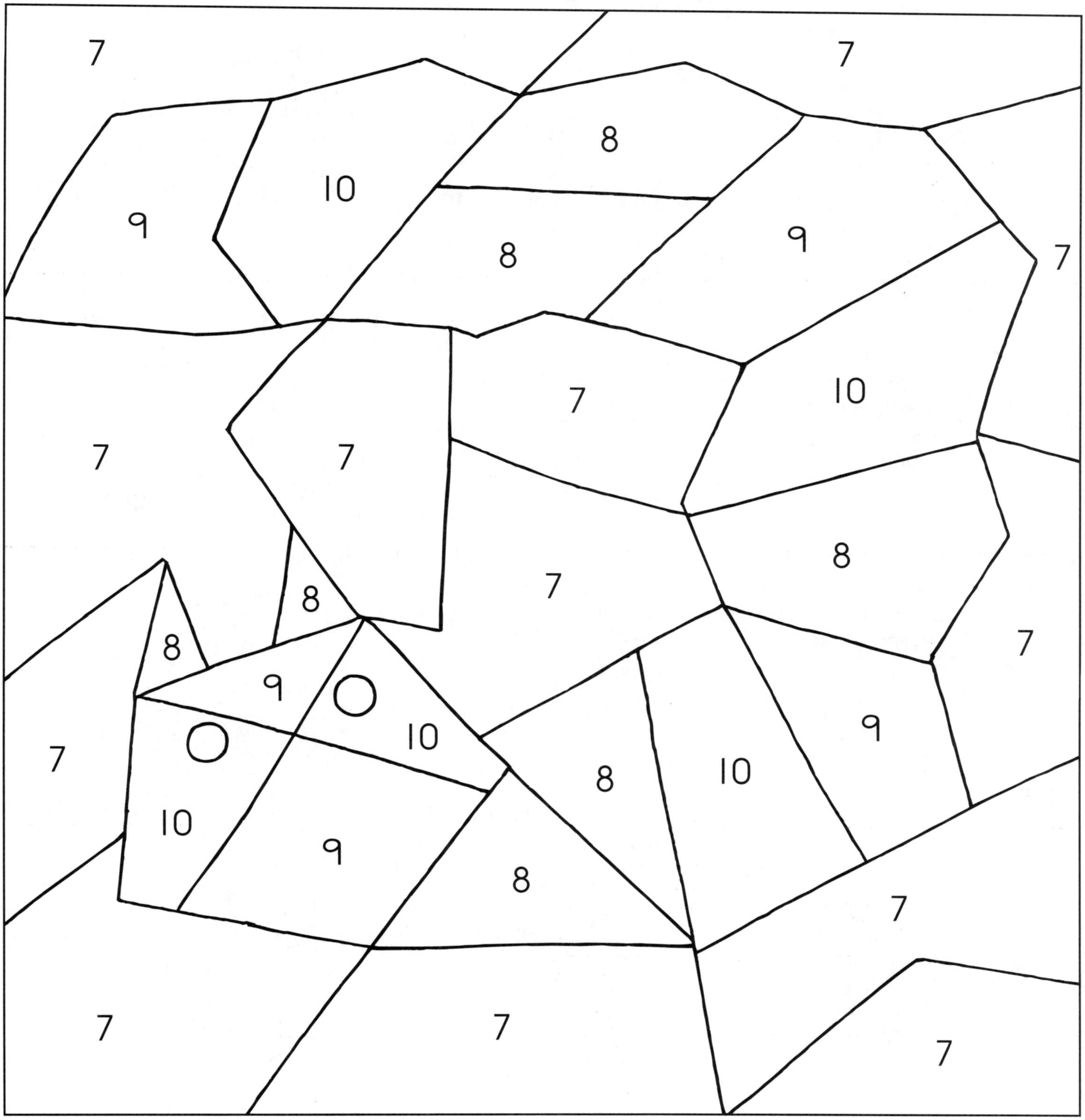

Related Activities

Literature List

Your students will enjoy these books about holidays.

Dragon Parade: A Chinese New Year by Steven A. Chin (Steck-Vaughn, 1993)

Kwanzaa by Deborah M. Newton Chocolate (Childrens Press, 1990)

Will There Be Polar Bears for Christmas? by Julia Jarman (Golden Books, 1994)

Light the Lights! by Margaret Moorman (Scholastic, 1994)

Light the Candle! Bang the Drum! by Ann Morris (Dutton, 1997)

Stopping by Woods on a Snowy Evening by Robert Frost (Dutton, 1978)

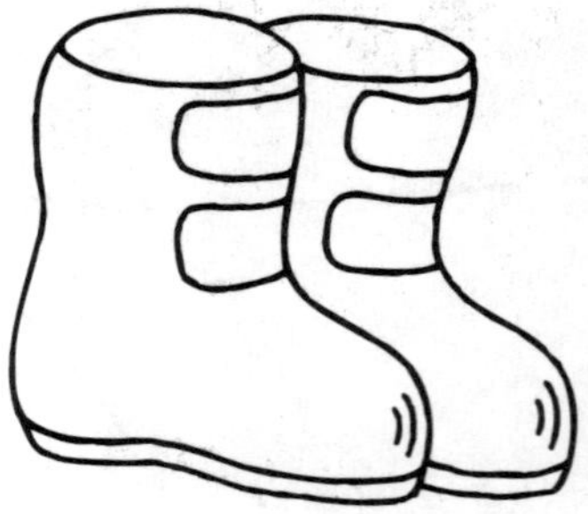

Language Development

The holiday season provides a feast for the eyes. Invite students to help you describe holiday sights.

- Describe a holiday-related object (such as a Christmas tree) and have the students guess what it is. Then let students take turns describing objects.
- Talk with your students about different ways light is used during the holiday season. As appropriate, introduce students to some of these words that are descriptive of light: shining, blazing, glowing, flashing, dazzling, flickering, shimmering, twinkling, gleaming, bright, and soft.

Writing

Writing thank-you notes is an excellent activity for helping students realize that the printed word has a purpose. It also helps students learn to be appreciative and thoughtful.

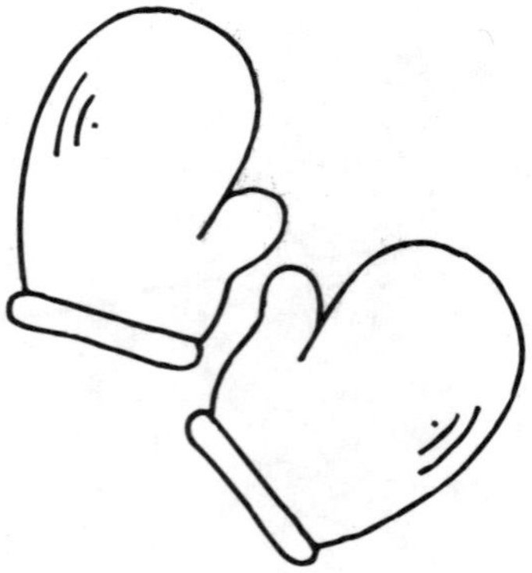

After the holidays, involve students in composing class thank-you letters to people who contributed to class holiday celebrations (for example, a parent who brought treats for the students). During other times of the year, students can compose class thank-you letters to the school custodian, cafeteria staff, and so on.